STAR WARS

BE MORE VADER

Written by Christian Blauvelt

Contents

Starting out 4
Perfect your interview technique 6
Succeed as an intern 8
Don't feel pressured by others' expectations 10
Find a mentor 12
Shoot for the stars 14

Getting established 16
Master the power of self-confidence 18
Control the conversation 20
Refine your negotiation skills 22
Don't bring problems; bring solutions 24
Present with confidence 26

Seeking promotion 28
Manage changing circumstances 30
Assess your competition 32
Insist on proper recognition 34
Make your requests with conviction 36
Devise a solid career plan and stick to it 38

Working with colleagues 40
Never tolerate insubordination 42
Lead by example 44
Hire external contractors if necessary 46
Make your expectations clear 48
Manage the talents of others 50

Becoming a leader 52
Accept a leadership position 54
Give credit where credit is due 56
Provide decisive and forthright feedback 58
Watch your back 60
Terminate contracts with immediate effect 62

Introduction

The dark path to success

You might be an apprentice, but you can master your own career—you just need drive, ambition, and connections. Climbing the corporate ladder is not that different from rising through the ranks of the Empire. Early mentoring will help you make your mark, whether it's seizing the initiative on a major project or hunting down rebellious Jedi. Developing a reputation as a ruthlessly efficient problem solver will fuel your progress, until you replace your mentor and assume the mantle of leadership.

Be More Vader provides essential advice to help you succeed at work. It will enable you to follow in the footsteps of the Dark Lord of the Sith—even if you don't possess the power of the dark side.

STARTING OUT

Success in the workplace has more to do with attitude than background. It shouldn't matter if your father is a Jedi or if you grew up on a backwater planet. Success ultimately depends on your ambition, resolve, and killer business instincts. Master these skills at the outset of your career and you won't be an apprentice for long.

"You were not summoned here to grovel, Director Krennic."
Darth Vader

Starting out

Perfect your interview technique

Stand out from the crowd in any interview by showing some backbone. Your busy interviewer probably has an inbox full of emails to which they must reply, budgets that need to be signed off, and rebellions to crush. Don't waste their valuable time by coming across as a weak-minded applicant or another corporate clone. Go in strong and fully prepared, and within 15 minutes even the most intimidating figure will be keen to hire you.

"My worthy apprentice... Where there was conflict, I now sense resolve. Where there was weakness, strength. Complete your training, and fulfill your destiny."

Supreme Leader Snoke

Starting out

Succeed as an intern

You can't get a job without experience, but you can't get experience without a job. So how do you get your boot in the blastdoor? Secure an internship by writing a sharp cover letter, playing up your eminent connections (a Sith Lord in your family tree can't hurt), or Force-fully rejecting your Jedi mentor. Once you've landed the job, arrive early, volunteer to answer phones and make photocopies, and show your total commitment by eliminating someone important to you.

"Let the past die. Kill it, if you have to.
That's the only way to become
what you were meant to be."
Kylo Ren

Starting out

Don't feel pressured by others' expectations

Everyone struggles at the start of their career, especially if they're under pressure to join the family business. Whether your grandfather was a Sith Lord, your mother helped "save the galaxy" with her strident activism, or your father was a scruffy-looking nerf herder who couldn't hold down a proper job, don't be afraid to forge your own path. It's fine to sever ties completely, even if that feels drastic.

"And you, young Skywalker. We shall watch your career with great interest."
Chancellor Palpatine

Starting out

Find a mentor

No matter how high your midi-chlorian count, you'll never get from entry level to Emperor on your own. You'll need guidance from someone who recognizes your talents and knows how to put you on the path to success. Networking is key: reach out via email or hologram to someone whose career you want. Then flatter them by asking advice on improving your prospects, be it making speeches, negotiating trade disputes, or firing lightning bolts from your fingertips.

"I am more powerful than the Chancellor... I can overthrow him. And... together you and I can rule the galaxy."
Anakin Skywalker

Starting out

Shoot for the stars

Dream big! You're at the start of your brilliant career and the whole galaxy is literally yours for the taking. Be suspicious of anyone attempting to hold you back, even if they are your one true love. Don't let them sidetrack you with lectures on right and wrong, pester you about family obligations, or criticize your ruthless streak. People who claim you have "changed" are simply intimidated by your meteoric rise to greatness.

GETTING ESTABLISHED

You've seized your early opportunities; now build that strong first impression into a formidable reputation. Organize and take control of meetings, inspiring your colleagues with your charisma, self-assurance, and take-no-prisoners approach. Discover how to command your peers' respect, but just know that the Death Star wasn't built in a day.

"The ability to destroy a planet is insignificant next to the power of the Force."
Darth Vader

Getting established

Master the power of self-confidence

Always be confident in your abilities. Your colleagues may possess better people skills, be proficient in the latest business software, or have even developed a moon-sized space station packed with planet-destroying weaponry. But the Force is strong with you, and you should never be afraid to demonstrate it. Underscore your status and presence with some subtle Sith mind games. Stand during a meeting while others sit—it's the ultimate power play.

"This bickering is pointless."
Grand Moff Tarkin

Getting established

Control the conversation

Keep your colleagues on a tight leash in meetings by silencing anyone who is derailing the conversation with small talk or pettiness. Wasting time is wasting money, so show them you mean business. Some colleagues, whether at the office or on your Death Star, may fuss over protocol or fight over turf—remind them that they are here to serve the Emperor. Assert your priorities with one swift stroke—how else will you deliver the Death Star on schedule and under budget?

"I am altering the deal. Pray I don't alter it any further."
Darth Vader to Lando Calrissian

Getting established

Refine your negotiation skills

You don't need to rely on Jedi mind tricks to become a dealmaker extraordinaire: focus your discussions on what both parties will gain in any negotiation. You may be coercing a local politician to carbon-freeze their best friend, but remind them how they'll win their city's autonomy in return. If they moan about the deal getting progressively worse as you increase your demands, bring in the muscle: stormtroopers are the best closers.

"My lord, is that... legal?"
Nute Gunray
"I will make it legal."
Darth Sidious

Getting established

Don't bring problems; bring solutions

No one likes a negative Neimoidian. There's nothing worse for starship morale than an individual who constantly focuses on problems or worst-case scenarios, and who cites legal niceties at every opportunity. Stay true to your vision and look for creative solutions to potential problems— before they arise. Assume a double identity and plunge the entire galaxy into a devastating civil war if you have to, but get the job done.

"All remaining systems will bow to the First Order!"
General Armitage Hux

Getting established

Present with confidence

Public speaking can be daunting, even for people in high-ranking positions. However, by having courage in your convictions and faith in your work, you will gain the confidence to address legions of your loyal subordinates. You can be guaranteed to make a strong impression by following these top tips: have a clear message, decorate the stage with a bold insignia, and project your voice. Make sure even the stormtroopers at the back can hear you!

SEEKING PROMOTION

Acknowledge and, more importantly, promote your achievements. If you're managing a heavy workload, training new staff, and keeping complex starship construction projects on schedule, make sure that your efforts are suitably recognized and rewarded. Learn how to ask for a promotion and ensure your demands are met.

"We must move quickly.
The Jedi are relentless."
Palpatine

Seeking promotion

Manage changing circumstances

At some stage in your career, you will face change at your workplace. It could mean staging a hostile takeover of a rival trade federation and toppling their leadership. Or it could mean a crucial rebrand when your Republic suddenly becomes the first Galactic Empire. Worse still, a management shakeup could mean redundancies, especially for your mystical, hooded colleagues. Find the opportunity in change and execute on it—or be executed from your current role.

"It's all Obi-Wan's fault!
He's jealous!
He's holding me back!"
Anakin Skywalker

Seeking promotion

Assess your competition

Rivalries can be healthy. They can make you stronger, sharper, and fiercer. The Sith say that even within a defined teaching relationship, the master should embody power while the apprentice craves it. However, the moment that rivalry starts holding you back, you need to eradicate it—show no mercy, even if you once considered your rival a brother. Don't let sentiment undermine your progress— a career that stops growing is a dead career.

"I've delivered the weapon the Emperor requested. I deserve an audience to make certain he understands its remarkable... potential."
Director Krennic

Insist on proper recognition

How you communicate your achievement is as vital as the achievement itself. Whether it's the impact of your brand on social media or the impact of your Death Star's superlaser on a planetary crust, your success will count for nothing unless your CEO or Emperor fully understands its worth. Make them understand it—then make them grasp *your* worth by demanding a higher position, with an appropriate pay rise. Advancement is never given; it is taken.

"The Republic will agree to any demands we make."
Count Dooku

Make your requests with conviction

It is imperative to show steely resolve during negotiations. Your business partners have staked their time, capital, and battle droids on your schemes, and they demand a commensurate return on their investment. These commercial allies will expect you to use their resources to make a lasting impression on the opposition. So never back down, even if that means feeding enemy negotiators to hungry beasts and starting a galactic war.

"Everything that has transpired
has done so according to my design."
Darth Sidious

Seeking promotion

Devise a solid career plan and stick to it

Your focus on progression needs to be as sharp and deadly as a lightsaber. In the short term, getting ahead could mean maximizing profits or recruiting a new apprentice. In the long term, it could mean taking 20 years to build a mighty battle station to help you manage an unruly galaxy through fear alone. You can't take your eye off the ball, especially if that ball is the Death Star—a monumental statement like that will ensure your abiding legacy.

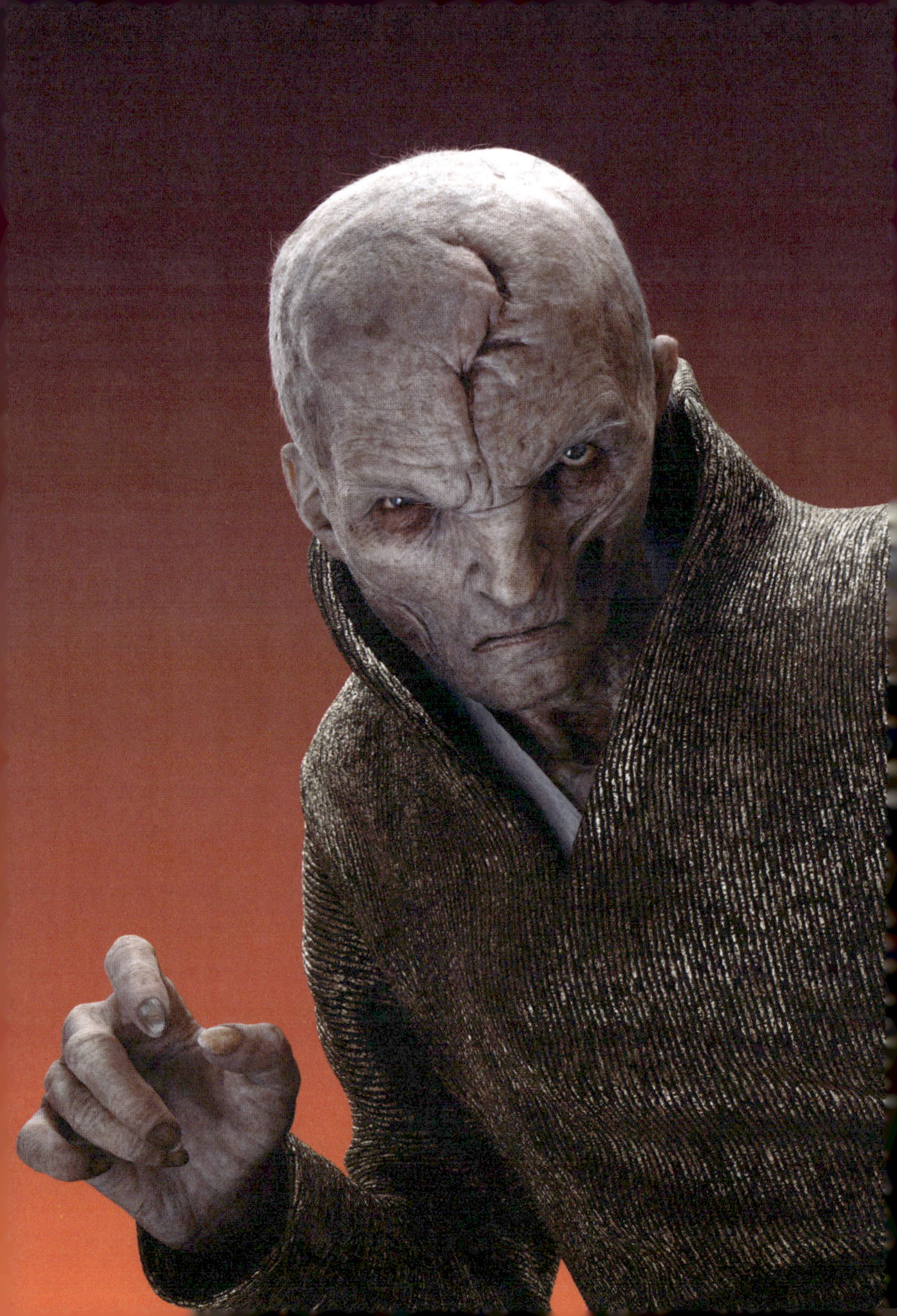

WORKING WITH COLLEAGUES

You're powerful with the Force, but even you can't do everything alone. You'll never build a new organization out of the ashes of a fallen Empire unless you instill new purpose in its former staffers and recruit new, highly motivated employees. Yes, this may mean getting inside their heads or bridging their minds, but that's a small price to pay for absolute power.

"You're a bug in the system."
Captain Phasma

Working with colleagues

Never tolerate insubordination

Some colleagues are determined to make you look bad. You may have taken them from their family when they were a child, given them a staff number instead of a name, and trained them only in combat—yet they're still ungrateful. If your co-worker is simply unmotivated, alert your manager or insist they submit their blaster for inspection. If they're outright rebellious, bring a righteous chrome fist down upon them.

"I'll take them myself! Cover me!"
Darth Vader

Working with colleagues

Lead by example

Sometimes, if you want something done right, you just have to do it yourself. Even the best TIE fighter pilot in the fleet could learn a maneuver or two from flying in attack formation with you. When you inevitably blast those rebel scum from the sky, remember to take all the credit for yourself. And if, in a one-in-a-million chance they slip away from you, then it's vital to have other people nearby to blame. Win-win.

"You are free to use any methods necessary..."
Darth Vader

Working with colleagues

Hire external contractors if necessary

There are times when your own team can't get the job done, so you might have to call in outside experts. External consultants could advise on organizational restructuring, while bounty hunters could use outside-the-box methods to track down a rebel ship. Your employees might sneer at these hired hands, but inhouse staff are less likely to look beyond established practices to find your quarry amidst floating garbage. Just warn the contractors not to disintegrate your prisoners.

"Asteroids do not concern me, Admiral. I want that ship, not excuses."
Darth Vader to Admiral Piett

Working with colleagues

Make your expectations clear

It's only natural to have high standards when you're a Force-sensitive, exceptionally powerful individual identified as the "Chosen One" in a galaxy teeming with billions of beings. Those around you will invariably struggle with matters that seem ludicrously simple to you. Be patient—up to a point—but make sure your instructions are crystal clear; don't give anyone a second opportunity to disappoint you.

"A cur's weakness, properly manipulated, can be a sharp tool."
Supreme Leader Snoke

Working with colleagues

Manage the talents of others

Deploy staff in ways that align their duties with their talents. Training and performance evaluation might come naturally to a chrome-armored operative who enjoys intimidating subordinates. Another underling's public speaking skills could inspire your assembled legions. And if a staff member displays raw, untamed power, set him loose on your enemies. While your employees benefit from professional development, you'll profit from realizing their full potential.

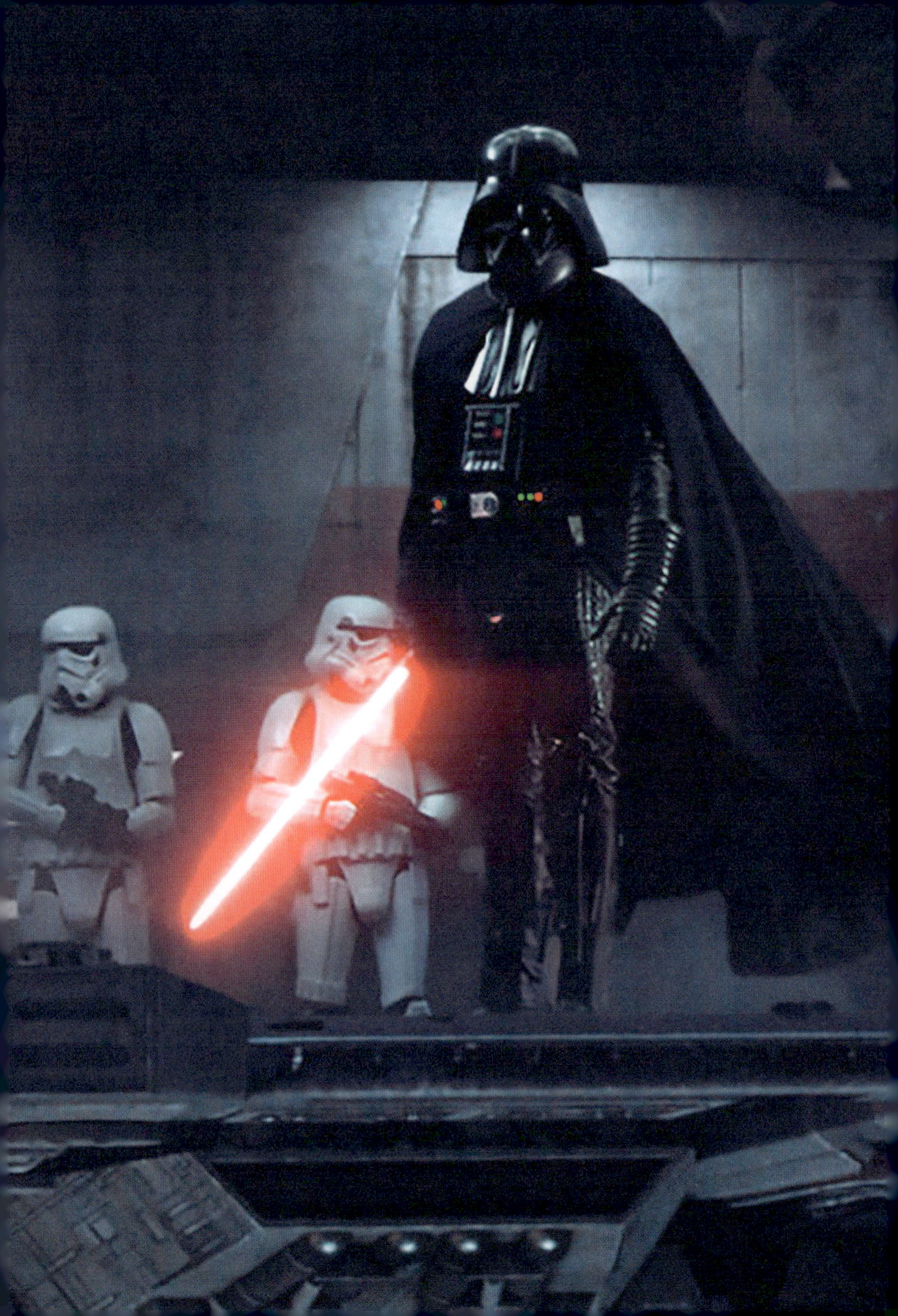

BECOMING A LEADER

The qualities that define great leaders can vary hugely depending on whether they are in charge of a start-up enterprise or a Star Destroyer. However, one attribute is vital: they must project an aura of authority and stability. Sow seeds of fear to motivate your team in the short term, if necessary, but for long-term leadership you must command their admiration and loyalty.

"When I left you,
I was but the learner;
now I am the master."
Darth Vader to Obi-Wan Kenobi

Accept a leadership position

Some individuals train for years to be a leader, while others become one overnight. If an opportunity arises, be prepared to seize it, whether it has been planned or appears from out of the blue. You may suddenly be called on to manage your team's response to a demanding client or lead a search party for stolen battle station plans. How you handle pressure during a crisis will determine whether you are true leadership material.

"You have been well-trained, my young apprentice. They will be no match for you."
Darth Sidious to Darth Maul

Becoming a leader

Give credit where credit is due

Your employees naturally look up to you and will thrive on your support, encouragement, and gratitude. Don't underestimate the impact of positive feedback, especially if you are asking a staff member to face a challenging assignment or deal with some meddling Jedi Knights. Boost their confidence, but always remind them who they have to thank for their advancement. After all, an apprentice is only as good—or bad—as their master.

"The Emperor does not share your optimistic appraisal... of the situation. ...And he is most displeased with your apparent lack of progress."
Darth Vader

Becoming a leader

Provide decisive and forthright feedback

You have risen to a position of prominence by meeting targets, advancing your organization's reach, and putting your life on the line when required. If your subordinates are unable to do the same, they deserve to face the consequences. That may mean a negative performance appraisal, a demotion, or having their prestigious project taken from them. You must find new ways to motivate your staff, because an Empire that tolerates failure deserves to be overthrown.

> "Remember back to your early teachings. All who gain power are afraid to lose it."
> **Palpatine**

Watch your back

Complacency is the enemy of a long career. Once you've reached the top, you will be vulnerable—having gained everything, you now have everything to lose. Strike first against those who seek to undermine you. That vice president you caught glaring sideways at you? Transfer them to another office. That aging apprentice lost in dreams of glory? Let another recruit strike them down. Know that any weakness will be exploited. Such is the way of the Sith.

"You have failed me for the last time, Admiral."
Darth Vader

Becoming a leader

Terminate contracts with immediate effect

Firing loyal staff is never easy. However, just because instant dismissal can be a painful experience for your employee, it doesn't have to be hard on you. There's nothing improper about remaining in your meditation chamber and using technology to pass on the message. It's fast and effective, and means you won't have to directly deal with the administrative nightmare of clearing out the stationery, pot plants, or bodies of incompetent, recently departed admirals.

Senior Editor Cefn Ridout
Project Editor Beth Davies
Senior Designer Clive Savage
Pre-production Producer Siu Yin Chan
Producer Zara Markland
Managing Editor Sadie Smith
Managing Art Editor Vicky Short
Publisher Julie Ferris
Art Director Lisa Lanzarini
Publishing Director Simon Beecroft

DK would like to thank: Sammy Holland, Michael Siglain, Troy Alders, Leland Chee, Matt Martin, Pablo Hidalgo, and Nicole LaCoursiere at Lucasfilm; Julia Vargas at Disney Publishing; Emma Grange for editorial assistance; Chris Gould for design assistance; and Julia March for proofreading.

First American Edition, 2018
Published in the United States by DK Publishing
1450 Broadway, Suite 801, New York, NY 10018

Page design copyright © 2018 Dorling Kindersley Limited
DK, a Division of Penguin Random House LLC
20 21 22 10 9 8 7 6 5 4 3 2 1
001-317165-Mar/2020

© & TM 2018 LUCASFILM LTD.

All rights reserved. Without limiting the rights under the copyright reserved above, no part of this publication may be reproduced, stored in, or introduced into a retrieval system, or transmitted, in any form, or by any means (electronic, mechanical, photocopying, recording, or otherwise), without the prior written permission of the copyright owner. Published in Great Britain by Dorling Kindersley Limited.

A catalog record for this book is available from the Library of Congress.

ISBN: 978-1-4654-7736-1

DK books are available at special discounts when purchased in bulk for sales promotions, premiums, fund-raising, or educational use. For details, contact: DK Publishing Special Markets, 1450 Broadway, Suite 801, New York, NY 10018, SpecialSales@dk.com

Printed and bound in China

A WORLD OF IDEAS:
SEE ALL THERE IS TO KNOW
www.dk.com
www.starwars.com